Just b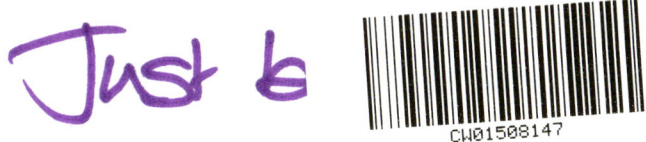

#LIFEBOSS

BE THE BEST VERSION OF YOU

ANDIE M. LONG

To vicky
love
Andie M.
Long
x

To

Francessca Webster

Thank you for the inspiration, your support, and for being a great friend.

Congratulations on following your own career dreams.

I wish you every future success.

CONTENTS

INTRODUCTION

Why this book?

I've always been a fan of self-improvement. Since way back when I've read books on how to improve your life such as Cheryl Richardson's *Life Makeovers* and more recently Gabby Bernstein's *The Universe Has Your Back*. Books with little projects that made me re-assess myself or check in with myself. I'll tell you straight off that this is NOT a book on how to look like a supermodel or become rich beyond your wildest dreams. If the latter of the two happens because of this book however, I'd love a pair of Louboutins.

This book is about making the most of what you have, while getting you to think about the things you'd like to reach for, so that you can work towards living a life you love. It's a book you can dip in and out of and do again as your life changes, which of course it will.

And being real there's a chapter on when life gives you lemons and why it's okay to go hide under the duvet once in a while.

I've wanted to write this book for years and indeed I started it a couple of years ago and then life went wrong. A two year period of ill health had me assessing everything, made my employment come under threat (I worked two days a week as a secretary) and basically had me hitting rock bottom.

What happened from there was transformational. I looked at what I could do, what skills I had outside of my day job. Something I could do from home and from my bed if my health continued to be challenging. I'm now self employed as a Book Editor (I'm also an Indie author with many published novels and novellas), leading a life I could only have dreamed of, yet this was at my fingertips all along - what I'd lacked was the courage to go for it. That nasty period of ill health led me to push for the life I wanted.

I'll talk more about my personal experiences as we go along, but just to say as we start this journey together that I'm an almost 47 year old mother from Sheffield, with a muffin top from eating too much Toblerone and an annoying anxiety disorder which can make me resistant to leaving the house. Whatever your background you can do the things in this book and hopefully end up with a little bit more of what you fancy in your life.

When I was eighteen I was hit by a car. This had a major effect on how I view life. I'm not a planner, I loathe having to make arrangements way ahead, much preferring to live for the day that I'm on. It's why I wake up in a morning and if my Dad says do I want to go out for lunch with him, I say yes. It's why my house doesn't look like a show home (much to my OH's chagrin).

As a comedy writer be warned of future silliness and sarcasm in the following chapters.

———

So here we are. You're about to turn the first pages of a new chapter - (get it!?)

All you need as you work through this book is a journal, a pen, and your enthusiasm.

This is the first book in my Lifestyle series. I hope you enjoy joining me on this new venture.

There is a Facebook group that runs alongside this book for daily motivation and inspiration: Here

Love, Andie xxx

IT DOESN'T MATTER
WHAT HAPPENED YESTERDAY.
TODAY IS A NEW DAY AND YOU
CAN CHOOSE ANY DAY TO
ASPIRE TO AN IMPROVED LIFE.

CHAPTER ONE

The Beauty of Journalling

To know how you are truly feeling in the present moment and to explore things you might want to change is not something easily done. After dismissing Journalling as mumbo-jumbo for a long while, it came as a shock to me when I started and actually discovered that it's probably one of the most useful things I've ever done in my life.

For me, journalling was introduced to me while on a writing course where we were asked to spend ten minutes every morning writing in a fresh note-book just for daily writing. Lots of people on the course including me asked the question, "About what?" The answer with journalling is that it doesn't matter what you start writing about. After so many minutes your subconscious will kick into gear and your thoughts and feelings will come tumbling out over the page. In my very first foray into journalling,

I sat in the garden, opened my beautiful, specially purchased notebook and with a coffee at my side I began. All I wrote for the first few sentences was how I felt that morning and I described where I was sitting. That led on to me talking about how lovely it was to be outside but that I wish I had a better office space inside the house. I wrote that my hopes were to write full-time one day but that it felt like a dream, like wanting to be a rockstar. Then my subconscious kicked in and I wrote the following:

I've written over ten books.
I'm already a rockstar!
I just need more people to know about them.

I finished my day's journalling by stating that it was time to view myself as a businesswoman and not a would-be author. My attitude was all wrong.

In only one session of journalling I'd identified my biggest problem with myself. A lack of self-belief. If I couldn't take myself seriously as an author who would?

Now let's put my feelings of inadequacy into context:

- I've had paid books go Top 350 in the whole of the Amazon store, out of millions.
- I made The Alphabet Game ebook free and it went to Number One in the whole Amazon chart.
- I had a friend request from one of my heroes - EL James herself.
- People read my books.
- People write to tell me they're awesome.
- People ask when the next one's coming out.
- Blogs both large and small feature MY books.
- People come to see ME at author events to purchase copies of my books and get my signature.

Writing these things down made me realise that I wasn't being fair on myself. Okay I wasn't a USA Today bestseller (yet!). Yes, there are much bigger authors out there than me. But instead of feeling sorry for myself, it took me to write it down to see that I was not being the best version of ME.

My journalling continues to this day. Yes, sometimes I miss a day or two, but I can tell you honestly, when I do I can tell.

My brain feels like strings of messy spaghetti.
I rush through the day.
I feel frustrated.

Those ten to fifteen minutes in a morning (I suggest with that morning drink, and if you don't have time, get up earlier), set me up for the day. My inner thoughts will come out onto that page and I will write until my intentions for that day are revealed, what the most important things to me right now are.

Note that Journalling is not the same as keeping a diary. In a diary you relate what's happened to you and keep a record of it for history. In a journal you write about events only if there's some purpose to it. For example, if you went to the gym and felt fat and frumpy and felt other patrons were bitching about you. In that instance you'd write about how that made you feel and then you'd explore ways you could work out that didn't make you feel this way, or how you were going to deal with the bitches. Journalling lets you release those creative ideas and reach for the stars.

ACTION

Time to get going! So the first things I want you to do are:

1. Purchase a journal that speaks to you. One you'll want to pick up every morning.
2. Purchase or choose a pen that writes really nicely. You know the ones, they glide across the page.
3. Decide where you'll write. A nice spot in the living room? A local QUIET coffee shop. I really do stress it needs to be somewhere that you can concentrate.
4. Agree to make that time for yourself most days. An appointment with your mind.

5. Write - or draw, or bullet point. Don't feel you have to write reams and reams of words. I go between writing pages of thoughts to drawing little thought bubbles and putting short thoughts in them.

I want you to journal for a whole week before moving onto any of the other exercises in this book. You need to spend the time letting your thoughts, ideas and frustrations spill out over the page. From there we can shape them up. Remember, things will evolve. Thoughts you have on day one, may have changed by the end of the month as you work things out in your mind and on the page. Remember what I said in my introduction, we're always changing. I will bet you that by the middle of the week you'll be itching with ideas of changes you want to make in your life, or you'll see how miserable some things are making you feel.

At one point when I first journalled and I wrote down what would be my ideal day I actually physically cried. A sign I really had tapped into my subconscious and emotions. So expect feelings to emerge. It's all good. Write them down.

Prompts.

In case you are struggling with what to write when you first start, I'd suggest focusing on the following:

- Why am I doing this (starting this journey)?
- What is frustrating me right now?
- What makes me happy? What do I love about my life?
- What are my dreams (don't limit yourself with reality, write whatever it is down).
- Where am I happiest - locations, eg on holiday near the beach, sitting in coffee shops with friends, walking the dog.

My own journalling experience on this week.

Immediately on Day One, I opened up on the page and wrote down the things that were niggling me right now. I had no idea until I did it just how much I had on my mind! This is from my journal:

I'm frustrated with feeling like I'm being lazy, with me having a sedentary job.

I feel I'm being lazy making work excuses for not doing housework.

I'm eating too much crap.

My skin isn't in the best condition and I keep scratching at it, especially my neck.

I've been so busy with work that I've found it hard to switch off and sleep at night, have been neglecting everything for work and getting a bit stressed by my workload (I overbooked myself this week with editing jobs).

I need to help my son with revision and I've not done it with being busy and because he keeps going out with his friends.

I'm not having any me-time because I use it as an excuse to do something book related, making me realise that because I love what I do I find it hard to break off from it to do anything else.

I want to get away for the weekends more.

I totally forgot to book myself any time off when I went self employed! So I've blocked two weeks at Christmas for no editing work.

I have a book I'm cowriting with another author which needs me to work on it so we can agree the direction of it. It needs my attention.

I'd still like a caravan, but it would need to have a sea view and be close to the beach.

I have a book commitment I now think isn't such a good idea and need to think of maybe withdrawing from the project as it doesn't seem well thought out. Maybe I could use that time to advance other projects.

All this came from just **fifteen minutes** sitting down with my journal. I've been doing this for years so be aware it will probably take you longer, don't rush the process.

WE HAVE ONE LIFE AND I'M GOING TO TAKE TEN MINUTES A DAY TO CHECK IN WITH MYSELF SO I CAN MAKE THE MOST OF MINE.

CHAPTER TWO

Another way to visualize your dreams - the mood board.

A couple of years ago I was miserable. Trying to become an established writer, working the day job, trying to keep the family happy, housework done. You get it. **I burned out.** I ended up taking 6 months largely away from social media and writing. I retreated to my happy place.

Except it wasn't.

What I'd done instead was stick my head in the sand and avoid what was happening.

I'd been doing too much.

Now I was running away (inside my own head).

Back to it all six months later and I had to start the writing game from scratch. I made a business plan. I had lots of releases coming up. I was **busy, busy and doing, doing**.

My day job got extremely stressful, my anxiety went sky high.

I got agoraphobia and couldn't leave my house.

Why am I telling you all this? Because it could happen to any one of us, when we're so busy trying to be Superwoman we forget **we don't actually have magical powers**. Plus when we do get to the end of each night, feeling drained and tired, have we done what **we** wanted to do, or have we been **people pleasing** all day?

At the time I was becoming run down, my life coach friend was running a free course and as part of that process we had to design a mood board. Now here's where you need to sit up and take note of what I'm proposing and not say "I don't have time for that mumbo-jumbo". Because **an hour spent today can change your life for the better**. How do I know? I've done it myself.

At the centre point of my first mood board was a statement saying that if I felt rubbish it was okay for me to spend the day in bed if I needed to. I did need to. I **gave myself permission to put my healing first**. I stopped giving myself grief over the fact I wasn't well. I ate the pretty cakes. I bought sunflowers and other cut flowers so I saw beauty and nature around the house. I stared out of the window a lot. I ate slightly healthier (I'm no saint). I didn't return to the yoga I used to love but instead started daily walks. The living room had a makeover and became a place I wanted to spend time in instead of somewhere that annoyed me every time I went in there. **The board gave me a focus**, pinned up in my spare room where I could see it daily.

Last year I re-arranged my spare room to give myself the **office space I'd always dreamed about**. The pic on the top left of the mood board was my inspiration. White desk, hints of blue and pink and yes I bought a fluffy pink cushion.

So then it was time to **make a new board** because **I'd begun to change**. I'd started to focus more closely on what I wanted for myself and was committed to work smarter towards those goals. I no longer saw myself as a secretary who wrote on the side. I was a **female entrepreneur,** a **Boss Lady**, (and I have a mug that says so).

At the time of writing I am on my third board. Every time I evolve and the board becomes my reality, I make a new one. It will soon be time for a fourth because I have new dreams and aspirations.

Right now on my third board is the following (the photo of the board can be found in the Facebook group):

A picture showing the benefits of dog walking to health.

A picture of a woman drinking coffee in a cafe.

A picture of a woman in boho clothing outside a caravan (my dream purchase)

A quote about looking back at where you came from to be proud about your progress

A motivational quote that says the universe is working a miracle and another that says my business gets better every day.

A picture as a reminder that I need to make time for myself (I can become a workaholic cos I love what I do)

A picture that says NO EXCUSES

Another that tells me not to force anything, just let things be.

A reminder that I love the beach.

As well as posting about career motivation I make sure my boards remind me that:

Relaxation time with a book is ESSENTIAL to my wellbeing.

Breathing fresh air each day is ESSENTIAL to my wellbeing.

ACTION

Make your own mood board. Think of the issues that have arisen for you in your journalling.

1. Open a word document and copy pictures over that resonate with what you enjoy, who you are, and who you want to be, or cut them from magazines. For example. Do you currently go to aerobics once a week because your friends do and actually you'd like to go running? Mood board the running pic.

2. Print the pictures off, stick onto some card and **place the mood board somewhere you will see it EVERY DAY**.

Make sure to have some fun with this too. If

you've an overwhelming urge to be an alien from outer space then pin a party picture where someone is dressed like one and plan your own!! Don't put blocks on yourself, this board is to help you **free** yourself.

There will be a point where you **review your mood board**, like I did, later in this book.

IF YOU ARE BREATHING
YOU ARE WINNING AT LIFE.
BUT IF YOU CAN, BREATHE
SOMEWHERE LOVELY.

CHAPTER THREE

It's all about those small steps, not a big leap.

Now you have your visual mood board it's time to look at **one** aspect of the board and think of **a small step towards it**.

For example, I had pinned a photo of a woman with well defined abs etc. She looked strong. I'm 46 with a middle-aged body. My small step towards this would be to increase the steps I take each day walking, so I'm building that strength. Hopefully this would lead to definition in my thighs and calves like on the picture. Once I've achieved this, I may start some work on another part of my body, perhaps adding in a few arm exercises with weights, but until I reach the first step, it's better not to think that far ahead, otherwise it will seem overwhelming, impossible and you'll risk giving up before you've even started.

With my home office, there were a lot of little actions before it was complete.

I had to:

1. Move the spare room furniture around to make space.
2. Order a new desk and chair.
3. Get my other half to assemble the new desk and chair! (I am no good at DIY).
4. Organise my notebooks, papers, pens etc.
5. Find a space for my laptop.
6. I bought a new noticeboard and pictures to make the space my own.
7. I even purchased a Boss Lady mug so that when I'm in that space I'm visually reminded it's to work!
8. The final piece was a rug.

So you see, lots of jigsaw pieces which then make up the whole picture. And I've continued to work on this space adding small touches to both improve and make the space mine and a place I want to be seated at. I surround myself with motivational tools such as my mood board.

My mindset has completely changed since I

journalled and did the mood board. I'm coming at everything from an 'ideal life' viewpoint instead of a 'life is a struggle' one. Despite knowing I have another operation ahead of me I'm being positive and making the most of every day, because each is a blessing. I could sit worrying and focusing on that operation and ruin the next few weeks until it takes place and believe me I have spent months in the past doing exactly this kind of thing. What a waste when a change of mindset could have made things so much better.

ACTION

1. Look at your board and write down in your journal one small step you can do towards each goal. Maybe if you have time write these out on some A4 paper,

decorate it and stick it up near your mood board.

2. Look at your board EVERY DAY and make sure you are doing that small step towards at least one of the pictures, making it become YOUR reality.

IF YOU SIT AND DO NOTHING
THAT'S EXACTLY WHAT YOU'LL ACHIEVE,
SO DO SOMETHING, NO MATTER
HOW SMALL, TOWARDS YOUR GOALS.

CHAPTER FOUR

Sometimes you have to give in and that's okay

I'm placing this chapter near the front for a reason. Sometimes life deals blows. It's life after all and we get ups and downs. Some days/months/years you're thrown curve balls.

It's okay to not be able to cope.
It's okay to be struggling.
It's okay to ask for help.
It's okay to go get in bed with a good book and leave your hubby in charge of the kids sometimes.

Obviously this book is generic and I don't have a crystal ball on your life or your support system, but just know that if you're struggling and you need help **please go get it or talk to a professional**. This is where I'm going to tell you some of my own background. I've had anxiety and depression since my twenties. Sometimes I've been unable to leave my house as my anxiety makes me quite agoraphobic. I struggle in social situations unless I know people - I find book signings a killer at first as I tend to ramble when I first get to them and believe people think I'm an idiot. Sometimes when I'm with people I freeze entirely and then I worry they think I'm a snob. Sometimes it's hard to fight that negative inner voice. When people find out I suffer with anxiety and depression they are always surprised because I'm usually a positive person with a smile on my face - and there's a good reason for that.

When I was 18 years old I got knocked down by a car. I always joke that it was because I wasn't drunk for once and so I wasn't seeing the road in double vision and it confused me. This accident had a profound effect on my life. To make the most of every day. Now by that I don't mean I spend every penny I have living in the moment, but if someone asks me out to lunch and the alternative is I was going to iron, my bag is grabbed and I'm out that door faster than you can shout "I'll have a margarita and a margherita."

Also some years ago now my family lost a close family member. My cousin was 22 when he passed away from an aggressive form of cancer. Despite his diagnosis he carried on making the most of his last days. He was an inspiration and I miss him beyond words. Again I was shown to make the most of life.

Sometimes people get confused and think they have to have achieved something amazing to prove their life has been worth it. Wrong. You just have to enjoy it. Enjoy the life you've been given, even if all that means is you have a thirty minute bath on a Friday night with decadent candles, you have a once a month date night, or you have a precious ten minutes read before you sleep every night. It's about being the best YOU can be.

With this in mind you have to realise that while you might be changing, you can't change other people unless THEY want it. If I decide I'd be happier if I had a date night every Friday night with my hubby where we indulge in great food and wine, I'm going to be frustrated and disappointed, because HE doesn't want to do that. He'd think it was a waste of money when we live across the road from the supermarket and can buy wine and pizza and sit in our lovely home. That leaves my choices as I can ask a friend if they want to go out, or I can get to the supermarket and look forward to a cuddle on the sofa after we've eaten. Don't try to impose what you want on other people. It doesn't work that way. You have to work within the parameters of realism!

WHEN I FIRST DECIDED I wanted to write this book a year ago, life decided it was time to give me a little reminder that ultimately I am not in control. I'd already been off work with anxiety and depression after a series of work-related events got me to the stage where one day I sat at my desk and thought 'I can't be here right now'. I walked out and got signed off by my doctor.

As I recovered from that I got a gynaecological infection resulting in more time off and extremely strong antibiotics which made my skin peel and become very sore.

Then I got a bout of food poisoning so bad that it lasted over a week and I spent days vomiting etc. I thought I was dying.

Bloods from the gynae tests showed I had high liver function tests. I didn't drink and it could have been caused by the super strong antibiotics but it warranted further investigation.

I was found on gynae scanning to have a polyp, a

fibroid, a fibroma and needed right ovary removal and another procedure.

Liver investigations revealed three polyps - my gallbladder needed to come out.

I WAS AT ROCK BOTTOM, my anxiety had flared up so much I was sitting on my sofa clock-watching for doctors appointments and was convinced I was going to die. The thought of going to hospital wasn't as bad as wondering why my liver function tests were abnormal. What was going on with my body? If I could just know and it was something small I'd have felt so much better.

(By the way, they never did find out why they went high.)

My gynae op went on hold while I did all my pre-op stuff for having my gallbladder out. I was finally on the first steps to getting things going again, getting my life back to normal...

Then eight days before the operation I broke my knee in two places when a dog tried to attack mine and my legs got trapped in the other dog's lead.

Now I was faced with everything being pushed

back at least twelve weeks. They were querying whether my leg would need surgery. After two days I was discharged with a leg brace and pot unable to do a lot of things for myself at first. My job, already under threat due to repeated bouts of sickness, now seemed impossible to get back to.

At this point I wondered if it was all a dream cos this shit couldn't possibly be happening to me, could it? Well yes it was.

I couldn't do my job.
I couldn't have my operations.
I was on pause.
Or was I?

I've said before, I love self improvement. So I got out my journal every day and wrote about **how shit my life was**. I got all my anger out. I journaled my worries and then I thought okay, if you had to leave your job, what could you do? I'm an author and author money is not guaranteed. You can have great months and poor months and I'm not a risk taker. I couldn't leave a regular job to just write books. I spoke to my sister and she said what about editing? I'd thought of this many times before and worried about sending a book out into the world with a massive plot hole or large error in it. In other words I'd held myself back **because of fear**.

Well, no more. I started saving motivational posts on Pinterest about being a GirlBoss (more on Pinterest later) and I looked into courses for editing and proofreading. I could study while I was stuck on the sofa with a broken leg, right? I passed the course and along with having a First Class Honours Degree in Creative Writing and being an author myself, I also spoke to my own editor, a great friend from my Uni days. "Do some for free" she urged me, "get some experience."

So I did. I did many, many free proofreads and edits while I was off sick and stuck. It gave me a focus so I didn't feel useless while I was sick and what was more - those authors said they'd use me, they wanted me as their editor. I sat back and thought, if I book X amount of books in for editing a month, alongside my writing income, I could go self employed.

And I did.

And so far, though I'm only a few months along, it's the best thing I ever did career wise and health wise. I work harder and more hours than ever, but in a job that works around my personality and health. If I don't want to see anyone, I don't have to. I don't have an hour's journey there and back from my place of employment. Because my author earnings are paid two months behind and I have to book edits in front I know that the few months ahead are okay. I made the leap and if it went wrong? Well I could temp. I have mad secretarial skills! But what I thought from all this was:

Maybe all that year of difficulties and challenge was to bring me to this place - doing exactly the career I dreamed off. Profound, but a nice thought.

I no longer dread Mondays and I no longer view Fridays as the end of the working week, but the pay off is sometimes because I tend to be a 100% or 0% person and I burn out, on those days I can crawl under the duvet in the middle of the day with a hot water bottle and a book and I'll think this is okay. I deserve time for myself, to rest.

SO WORK with your current situations. Maybe you'd be a lot less stressed if your food could be home delivered but your hubby doesn't want to pay for home delivery. Well write him a shopping list and ask which he'd prefer - he can fetch it or you'll order it!

Do you feel guilty for sticking your kids in front of the TV? If it means an hour with your kindle and that after that you won't feel fried, which would usually lead to you being short tempered with those very same kids, then do it.

You can't change life but you can change how you deal with it.

ACTION

1. Grab your journal and write down every single thing that is pissing you off. Leave a few lines clear underneath each one.

2. With a different coloured pen (and at a later time if you prefer), go back to each one and write what YOU can do to

improve that situation. If it's beyond your control then write that down, something like: *I cannot change this situation therefore I have to make my peace and accept it and I will do that by...*

3. Journal how you are going to invoke those changes in your life.

YOU CAN'T CONTROL LIFE,
BUT YOU CAN CONTROL HOW YOU VIEW IT.
VIEW IT WITH POSITIVITY IF YOU CAN.
IF NOT, BUY SOME CHOCOLATE
AND HAVE A DUVET DAY.

CHAPTER FIVE

Start from where you are
RIGHT NOW
and Balance the Scales.

At this present moment, some things that were out of reach to me a year ago are now within reach. I can make a choice right now to take on an extra piece of editing work, additional to what I **NEED** to earn per month and buy myself a treat with that money, maybe a designer handbag. I don't have to, but I could.

But years ago I had six pieces of clothing hanging in my wardrobe.

Your goals have to be realistic and focused on who you are **NOW** and where you'd like to be in the **FUTURE**.

Right now I can take on that extra piece of work because my OH is at work and my son is out with friends. But doing so would mean my free time is filled with work - so which do I want - the designer handbag or my feet up with a book? (Answer: depends on my mood lol).

Years ago when my son was small I would have turned overtime down to spend time with him, knowing these moments are precious. I was of the opinion that as long as bills could be paid and we could be fed, the rest didn't matter. We didn't need holidays, meals out, an abundance of toys. I would take my son around the car boot. It would be an outing on a Saturday walking in the fresh air. He'd get toys for a fraction of the price of what they are in the shops. I would buy kid's tired old Barbie dolls, bring them home, do them up and sell them on eBay - it paid for Christmas.

So, if your goal is to **EARN MORE** and that means **WORK MORE**, what's the **DOWNSIDE**? Is there one?

You need to **balance the scales**.

EXAMPLE:
Let's say you want to save for a family holiday:
WORK ONE EXTRA DAY TO EARN MORE = FAMILY HOLIDAY = MEANS ONE DAY LESS SPENT WITH FAMILY A WEEK.

So to get a week's holiday you're going to see the family approximately 52 days less? Does that balance the scales?

GET A JOB THAT EARNS MORE = FAMILY HOLIDAY

Does this **balance better**? **Absolutely**.

ACTION

Review your goals so far. Is what you want right now balanced? If not can you do this another way, or is it better to wait to pursue this goal?

SOMETIMES IT'S NOT THE
RIGHT TIME. IT DOESN'T
MEAN IT'S NOT IN YOUR FUTURE,
IT'S JUST NOT FOR RIGHT NOW,
AND THAT'S OKAY.

CHAPTER SIX

Comparing yourself to others

Rule number one in being the best version of you is knowing you are unique - there is ONLY ONE YOU!

By all means take that Sienna Miller hairstyle picture to the hairdressers (I do!), even take note of a little of her style (yep, still talking about me here, I have a little boho vibe going on), but then use this alongside your **own** style (mine is the just got out of bed look!). Work it baby!

What makes you, YOU? Your **Personality** list. Mine is below as an example.

1. I have a great sense of humour and a talent to make people laugh.
2. I have days where I work like crazy, versus others where I need to lie down all day - 0% or 100% - I have no in between.

3. I get anxious.
4. I love a coffee in a morning.
5. I adore chocolate.
6. I am competitive and ambitious.
7. I'm enthusiastic.
8. I will help people anyway I can within reason (don't ask me to do your ironing, it's never going to happen.)
9. I like acting silly and don't give a fig what you think of it (yesterday I bought me and the dog matching jumpers).
10. I'm that laid back I'm horizontal but don't be fooled I'm a pushover - if you incur my wrath you would know about it.
11. I have a Shit List for those who did 10. You don't want to be on it.
12. I find exercising really hard.
13. I love the sunshine and outdoors is where I'm happiest in the fresh air on a sunny day.

Now we're going to move onto the things we **envy** in others. Grab that journal again. Once again mine are posted below as an example.

1. I like to see people looking healthy, who have that glow.
2. When I see those yoga bodies with the really taut asses I get very jealous.
3. When someone gets a book deal I go green with envy.
4. When people post photos of themselves on a sunbed I want to go.
5. When I see lots of top authors supporting each other and doing amazing I wish they were my friends and sharing my books to what I presume are their bajillions of readers.
6. When I see pictures of house interiors looking sensational, I look around at my house and sigh.

ACTION

Make your own two lists as above. Following my example below write your way out of your 'comparisonitis'.

Firstly, go through your **envy** list above in light of your list of **qualities** and write a sentence underneath that gets rid of this envy. Eg,

1. I like to see people looking healthy who have that glow.

Using my personality: The chances of me having this glow naturally when I'm the colour of milk and so white the sun reflects away from me is remote, but **being a lazy arse who likes to sit on the sofa** means I could buy and apply a nice fake tan and fake it. Plenty of time for it to dry while I'm on the computer working! The advantages of this are I'd feel a bit better about myself and this might make me more motivated to try and be a little healthier for real and perhaps walk more on a sunny day to get it for real. Or if I remain my lazy ass self I'll be a nice golden colour, though probably with lots of streaks and stained bedsheets.

Moving forward: buy fake tan.

2. When I see those yoga bodies with the really taut asses I get very jealous.

Using my personality: I either decide to start doing yoga again, which I used to AND other exercise because that tight ass doesn't come from just yoga alone, or I face the reality that a compulsion to eat Toblerone and sit on the sofa a lot means I need to forget it.

I can use my **competitive personality** to go for it. All I need to tell myself is people would believe I couldn't do it and fire myself up.

NOTE: Yesterday I found a fabulous notebook in the shop which is a food doodle journal. You do things like draw the contents of your fridge. This is exactly the kooky kind of thing that would get me motivated as it's that little bit different. Find your mojo motivator.

Moving forward: Get the yoga stuff out. Try 20 mins once this week OR realise it's never going to happen and stop looking at these pictures.

3. When someone gets a book deal I go green with envy.

Using my personality: Okay Andie. Have you applied to agents to seek a book deal?

No?

What's that again? No? NO. You haven't tried to get one yourself. WTF????

Andie you cannot be jealous of someone who has aimed for something you haven't. Be jealous by all means if you applied to fifty agents and not a sniffle of interest, but none - well none since you started self pubbing in 2014. Go away and quit moaning, fire up that **enthusiasm** and write a book that could be on a shelf in Waterstones and submit it!

Moving forward: Submit it or quit it!

4. When people post photos of themselves on a sunbed I want to go on holiday.

Using my personality: Can you afford a holiday? Book one.

If you can't wait for the nice weather and grab that holiday book and head for the sunlounger. Remember you find it a **mood boost**. Grab a can of pina colada from the local supermarket. Do some extra work if needs be if you're in 100% mode. Or embrace your laziness and stick the central heating on, lay on the sofa and visualize the beach!

Moving forward: Start a holiday savings fund.

5. When I see lots of top authors supporting each other and doing amazing I wish they were my friend.

Using your personality: I met one of these authors at a signing the other week. She had the personality of a brick and that is being unkind to bricks. Again, what you see is what they want you to see and I ALREADY have lots of friends, who are worth one hundred times these people. If I'm meant to ever know any other authors it'll happen. Can't force friendships. Also you like to **help other people**, so maybe reach out to someone not doing as well as you who might see YOU as someone to envy and encourage them and support them.

Moving forward: Celebrate the friendships you already have and scroll on past what sometimes is a fake projection of personalities.

6. When I see pictures of house interiors looking sensational, I look around at my house and sigh.

Okay Andie, when was the last time you thought about decorating or even spring cleaned? Okay, enough said. Think: **laid back, coffee drinking, chocolate eating**. Likelihood of decorating yourself: 0%.

Moving forward: Collect photos of interiors you like. Pick a room you'd like to redecorate and make a list of what needs doing. Discuss with the other half. Make a new list of what he will allow after he tells you that no way are you having a life sized poster of Theo James on the back wall.

Finally, it's time to go **back** through the list of what makes you, **YOU**. I want you to make yourself a poster, draw a picture in your journal, or buy a tee shirt that sums up how awesome you are or some of what makes you, YOU.

Eg: I've bought a Pusheen tee from Primark - on the front it shows a Pusheen unicorn with 'aspiration' on it. On the back is a sleeping Pusheen with 'reality' on the back. My nickname is Pillow for a reason.

My poster would be:

I'm just a crazy, lazy-assed girl who loves coffee, Toblerone, and books.

It's time to treat yourself for being the uniquely awesome person you are. What simple thing do you love? Do it now. You earned it for being YOU.

Suggestions

A bath

A thirty minute read

A bar of chocolate

Five minutes with your eyes closed just breathing.

WHAT PEOPLE LET YOU SEE
ISN'T NECESSARILY THE TRUTH.
DON'T COVET OTHERS.
BE AN ORIGINAL.

CHAPTER SEVEN

Manifesting
The WooWoo chapter

It doesn't ultimately matter whether you believe you can ask the Universe for what you want or not. The power of manifesting can still be a tool you can use.

Manifesting is to put out into the universe what you would like. It's **NOT** a shopping list. Basically it's changing your thought processes to attract things to your life.

For example: at the end of October 2016 I was stuck. My books weren't selling as well as they could and I didn't know any new ways of marketing. I needed help. I sat thinking about this. That I could really use a mentor, someone at the next level who could guide me. At that point I was on the cusp of stopping publishing. I couldn't stop writing but it was becoming an expensive hobby. I'd gone from overnight success to an author whose sales hit with a bang and then fizzled right out. There was no longevity and it was costing me more to publish the books than I was earning.

At that time I saw a competition from a woman whose work ethic had come to my attention. She just seemed the most genuine, nicest person and every time she posted I read it. She was going to mentor three people and asked people to apply. I did it and forgot about it.

In November a friend messaged me to tell me I'd won. I was one of the three. This woman showed me the steps (she didn't do it for me, just showed me) to make my books sell better. Her method? To give away thousands of copies of my books for FREE. The old me, a part of me went *Free? Are you out of your mind? (resistance)*, but a louder part of me said *it's three months, what do you have to lose when your sales aren't all that anyway? (surrender)* So I went for it, I followed her advice and guess what? I sold more books. I became more knowledgeable about the market and what to write and how to release it. By the end of the three months I had a system I still use today.

But that wasn't all that happened - someone approached me about co-writing, other opportunities came my way. I worked harder than ever but I started earning again. I had success again. I then passed on my knowledge to other people so that they could benefit just as I had.

I wrote in my journal in October that I wanted to earn xx a day. By January this was happening so I doubled the figure in my journal. By February I'd doubled it. By March I was thinking is this really my life? Since then my earnings are like a rollercoaster but I manifest to this day. But the main thing is to visualize what you want and trust that if this is meant for you, the universe will make shifts to help you make it happen, but you have to believe and surrender (and there's my woo-woo bit).

So:

If I want to be happy, then I do things to make myself happy - happiness attracts more happiness.

If I want to learn about Facebook ads, I'll think oh it's time to explore that now. Last week I started an ad and within 3 days I had another author offer to show me how to do them and a section appeared in a course I'm doing on how to compose your Facebook ad pic. The exact things I'd been struggling with were suddenly answered!

FOR ANYONE who **doesn't believe in manifesting** you can still use the **principles**. Say you want to be more successful and you focus on that for yourself. Maybe you then carry yourself in a way that shows people you mean business and that attracts the right kind of people to you? Maybe when you're asked to do something you consider this against what you want. Don't offer to help someone tidy their wardrobes if you want to design their garden.

The main phrase I hear with manifesting is to act as if you already have what you want and I really do believe this, but it has to be within reason. It doesn't mean remortgage the house to buy a Rolex because you want to be super rich, but to wear an air of confidence will go a long way into being the best version of you.

ACTION

Spend five minutes every evening visualizing yourself as the person you are going to be. How do you feel? What are the smells, the sounds around you? How do you look? Where are you?

Keep this feeling around you for as much of the day as you can until life starts getting in the way! Look out for 'opportunities' coming your way that could move your vision for yourself forward. Don't let them pass you by, they are being sent because you asked for them!

IF MANIFESTING AND
VISUALISING ARE FREE,
THEN WHAT WOULD IT
COST YOU TO TRY?
EXACTLY.

CHAPTER EIGHT

Pinterest
and the value of pinning regularly.

If you have access to a computer and the Internet and you've yet to discover Pinterest, then get ready to lose hours out of your day!

Pinterest: www.pinterest.co.uk is basically a mass of 'pins' - information and photos, that you can pin to online boards. Your boards can be public or secret. Here's a step by step guide on how to pin once you've signed up. I've made a board for the readers of this book where I'll pin motivational things to it for you all! You can find it: Here

1. Head to Pinterest and sign in.
2. Click on your circular image at the top right hand corner and then on PROFILE
3. Click on BOARDS
4. Click the red plus sign.

This will bring you up a box that says CREATE BOARD.

5. Give your board a name. In this case I'm calling it LIFEBOSS: THE BEST VERSION OF YOU.

6. Do you want it secret or not? In my case I want it public.

You'll be given the option to add a description and a category. Sometimes it's hard to decide on a category. The nearest I could think this belonged to was HEALTH AND FITNESS.

7. Save.

8. Start pinning!

To pin you can search in the bar at the top of the page for anything you are interested in. You can pick a category and look through that. There are also POPULAR and EVERYTHING categories so you can browse there. Eventually Pinterest learns what kind of things you are pinning and puts them in a feed for you. Anything your Pinterest friends pin may appear here too.

I would suggest that you at least make one board and call this MOOD BOARD or INSPIRATION and place any pins that inspire you, anything that resonates with your dreams or those small steps you are taking. Keep adding pins but don't forget to look at the ones you have pinned and look for those hints as to what your current mindset is. You can tell a lot by WHAT you are pinning. If it's lots of diet foods then are you wanting to lose weight? If it's quotes about life being hard then you need some TLC right now. If its 17 pictures of Theo James, welcome to the time wasting talent of Pinterest! (I *may* have a sexy men board, ssh!)

I like to do a little pinning just before bed time. It helps me relax as it's very visual after a day of words, and it gives me motivation for the following day.

A PIN A DAY
KEEPS LACK
OF MOTIVATION
AT BAY

CHAPTER NINE

Thinking time
A Place of Space

Sometimes we need **space** and **silence** to think about what we want or to discover what's on our minds. I used to find that whenever I was blocked about something, without fail when I was on the bus going to work is when it would come to the fore and ideas would spring to the front of my mind. Basically that hour long bus journey was a time where I couldn't do anything else but sit there and think and so my mind used that opportunity.

Now I rarely get a bus, but I do love a shower. Now I find I can be in the shower for an extra fifteen minutes because I'm lost in my thoughts. (Once I had a Eureka moment for a plot twist and had to leave the shower, then dripped water along the floor to get to my room to write it down!)

Sometimes to clear my head I walk the dog.

The next time you're feeling stuck, try to find

your **place of space.** Go walk, shower, travel, and don't deliberately think of anything. Just let your thoughts come unbidden and see what happens.

But **please** have a notebook and pen on you, just in case those thoughts appear!

SOMETIMES THE ONLY
THINGS YOU NEED IN LIFE
ARE A LITTLE
PEACE AND QUIET.

CHAPTER TEN

Make things around you beautiful

Sometimes just the littlest things can make you feel better. (No, that's NOT what I meant, you naughty person).

I love flowers but in the winter I don't get to see my garden as much. Occasionally buying myself a bunch of flowers to put in a place I'll see often brightens the space and my mood.

Some suggestions are:

One special mug to put your hot drink in.

A hot water bottle for cold days, maybe with a fluffy cover.

A blanket.

A photo frame with a photo of loved ones or an inspiring place.

A comfy jumper.

A luxurious scarf for cold days.

Fluffy bed socks.

Treat yourself to a magazine.

A new notebook and pen.

Paint your nails with a new varnish.

Sometimes just tidying and cleaning can make you feel happier once you sit back and look at that lovely fresh space. (Personally I prefer sitting on the sofa with a hot water bottle and a drink from a favourite mug, but when I do make the effort I enjoy the freshness!).

As I mentioned in Chapter Two, I revamped my home office. It's the tiniest corner of my spare room, but I bought the most gorgeous, inexpensive cream chair, a tiny rug for underneath a white desk, and rose gold accessories. I love it. Just looking at it gives me a buzz and I love working at my desk now it's so pretty.

What small thing could you do today to make your surroundings more lovely?

HOW COULD YOU
FAIL TO FEEL HAPPIER
WHEN SURROUNDED BY
THINGS YOU FIND
BEAUTIFUL?

CHAPTER ELEVEN

Monthly review

As I've said before, this book can be started at any time. It's not a book simply for January 1st. At the end of each month I would suggest you review the month before and here are some suggestions and prompts on how to do that.

Copy the questions below into your journal.

1. Reviewing your journal from the past month, what were the three biggest themes that came up?
2. What steps have you taken so far to be the best version of you?
3. Does your mood board still reflect what you are trying to achieve/have achieved or do you need to update it?
4. What is the ONE aim you want to work towards most over the NEXT month.

5. What steps can you take to achieve this aim. (Write down both small and large).

6. What is the most realistic and achievable step that you will do at the beginning of this following month?

7. What will your reward be for achieving this step?

8. How do you feel after this first month of assessing your life and how to be the best version of you? Has anything surprised you?

ACTION

Now start a brand new page of your journal and write out the aim you wrote for number four in large letters over the page. Feel free to decorate it with inspiring photos or doodles or make yourself a poster for your office wall or noticeboard.

I HAVE THE POWER
WITHIN ME TO
DO THE MOST
AMAZING THINGS.

CHAPTER TWELVE

Have you met resistance yet?

By now you should have spent at least a month working on the best version of you. If not, just carry on for now journalling until you get past a month and then do your review. Ready now for the next part? Okay, let's go!

The chances are that one thing you really want, that appears on your mood board or in your journal is something that you are resistant to undertaking.

It's natural to have a resistance to change or a lack of confidence in taking a leap.

I wanted to be self-employed. It took me to almost lose my job for me to make this happen, yet this was in my power all along. At any point I could have trained as a book editor and set myself up in business, but my resistance came from the following:

Other half and family members: How can you

leave a regular job with a pension? (**outside pressure**)

Myself: What if I make a mess of it? (**self-doubt**)

This book has met my resistance:

Why would anyone want to read my ideas about life? (**self doubt**)

Who am I to advise people? (**lack of confidence**).

Again, you have to go back to listing your resistance and answering your own questions.

How could I leave a regular job with a pension?

My answer should have been that I wasn't the main breadwinner and could temp with my secretarial skills. Therefore I should have given it a try before. My pension is worth little and I can take out a private one.

What if I made a mess of it?

What if (and this is what happened), I make a roaring success of it?

If I made a mistake I'd correct it and apologise and... move on.

Why would anyone want to read my ideas about life (and this is why I HAVE published it).

The last twelve months have turned my life

around in unexpected ways. I've hit rock bottom and swum back up again. Life is not a straight line, it has many loops and curves and I can share my story and hopefully inspire other people. I've had depression and anxiety and can share my story of that and hopefully help people. I can motivate people to make the best of themselves and if this happens to just ONE person, then the book was worth writing.

Who am I to advise people?

People are always asking me for advice. Via FB messages, coffee with friends. I've read self help and motivational books for years and worked out my own ways of doing things. Why not share this?

Why not me?

Write in your journal the thing you are resisting. Why are you resisting it? After writing down all the reasons, write another sentence or two arguing against your resistance.

Are you now ready to make the change, or are you right to be resistant? There are no right or wrong answers. Just listen to your gut on these.

IF I DON'T TRY,
I DEFINITELY CAN'T
SUCCEED.
SO I'LL TRY,
ONE SMALL STEP
AT A TIME.

CHAPTER THIRTEEN

Keeping it real

This morning my dog was ready for her walk. I put on my lovely winter coat, hat and scarf; and decided that this would be the morning I'd use my brand new travel cup. I filled it with warm coffee, and dog lead in one hand, coffee in the other, I got to the door. My mirror image showed Instagram perfection, the perfect look of got-it-together woman. Had I got a camera on my phone (son currently has it), I'd have snapped a selfie and posted it for all to see.

As I walked outside I had to put the coffee mug in my pocket so I could lock the door.

I walked down the street and it was soooo cold.

I had a few sips of coffee as the dog trotted beside me - perfection. As I continued to walk down the hill I was all 'Wow, this is the life. Look at me with my shit together'.

Then the dog decided to do her business.

I put the coffee mug in my pocket again as it was windy and I needed to concentrate to get my dog's deposit into the poop bag.

As I bent down, my coffee mug upended from my pocket, landed upside down on the path and the coffee started to spill out over the pavement. The wind proved my victor and I ended up putting everything on the floor so I could get the flipping poop bag sorted out.

From shit together to shit all over in minutes.

Lesson to be learned: at any moment when you're celebrating something great, shit might happen. It's life and life deals in great stuff and crap.

I WILL NOT LET MY DAY BE RUINED
BECAUSE ONE SMALL
THING WENT WRONG.
MY MIND IS MY OWN.
I CHOOSE TO BE HAPPY.
A LITTLE BIT PISSED-OFF MAYBE,
BUT MAINLY HAPPY.

CHAPTER FOURTEEN

Grow down

When did life get so serious?

I'm constantly being told that I'm a laugh, a nutcase, make people giggle. I just let my hair down and don't allow people to dictate what I can and can't do (within the law that is!)

I could embrace my brainy First Class Honors Degree self (and sometimes I do, especially when I'm in business-mode), but life is so much more fun when you're smiling.

So don't grow up - grow down (at least occasionally).

Anyone who follows me on Instagram might have met 'Barbie Andie'. This started as a complete giggle when I realised that the real-life author me wasn't for Instagram worthy photos - picture the scene: tired face, huge eye bags, hair in a top knot and wearing of pjs. So I got a representative - a

Barbie doll. After a few posts I decided I was being stupid and stopped it. What happened?

I had messages.

Where was Barbie Andie?

You see, we all need a little crazy in our lives, so now and again Barbie Andie resurfaces.

ACTION

Grow down for a while! It's so freeing.

Try the following:

Buy a colouring book. NOT ONE FOR ADULTS. Or a dot-to-dot. Spend an hour doing it.

Put some music on and dance. Sing along. Do children care what they look like or do they try to do the performance of their lives?

Watch a Disney film.

Meet a friend and go around a funfair. Play hook a

duck and go on the ghost train and scream like crazy.
Touch the side of your friends face and howl with
laughter when THEY scream like crazy.
Play snap.
Blow raspberries at your other half every time he
speaks. Laugh as he gets exasperated.

Anyone tell you to grow up? Think about who's
being miserable and who's having fun. Smirk to yourself and carry on.

YOU KNOW WHAT?
TODAY I'M GOING TO
ACT MY SHOE SIZE,
NOT MY AGE.

CHAPTER FIFTEEN

If it wasn't difficult everyone would be doing it

Anyone jealous of my 'success' is more than welcome to come study the four years of highlights and cock-ups thus far, complete with its 14-16 hour days and times of tearing my hair out versus elation of things going good. Rollercoaster remember? Sometimes it's easy to take things at face value and not dig deep.

Something that may come up for you when you are changing things is guilt.

Many years ago me and my partner talked about the possibility of going to Australia. My hubby is a nurse and lots of nurses were making their moves that way. Embracing life's opportunities I'd said I'd consider a year and I even went so far as to see if I could have a career break.

In the end my OH was put off by the thought of the heat as another nurse who moved there had complained of their lethargy and constant showers.

It's hard to know if we would have gone because there was one thing tethering us to where we already were.

Our parents, siblings and friends.

But here, again, you have to do the balance equation. Mine would have been not physically seeing my family for a year, versus the benefits it could have brought to my son's life.

We did our equation, in this case it went no further than the temperature! We stayed home.

But there's a programme on the television *Escape Down Under* and every episode they show the family back home, nearly always crying 'Don't leave me.'.

Were these families prevented from doing what they wanted?

Guilt is a horrible emotion but I'll remind you. You have **one life**. Make the most of it.

Other people making you feel guilty should not stop you from pursuing your dreams. It's all about **balance**.

TODAY I WANT TO
OPEN MY CAGE AND
FLY AROUND A BIT.
THANK YOU FOR
UNDERSTANDING.

CHAPTER SIXTEEN

Sometimes you need to declutter elsewhere before your mind

Ever have that feeling when the house is a little upside down or you have piles of paperwork around where you feel a little icky, a little upside down, hassled?

I have it right now. There are Christmas decoration boxes around, presents waiting to be delivered, washing waiting to be sorted into piles, ironing to be put away, a bank statement needs checking. Everywhere I look there are things that need sorting and right now it's driving me mad.

The thoughts in my head are:

There's not time to do all this.

Ugh it's just chores everywhere I look.

It's never ending and the minute I do one task another appears.

Sometimes it's better just to set some time aside to clear up. To declutter. You can start with just one room. Once I've sat and worked out the bank state-ment and shredded the receipts I feel so much better in my mind. It gives me the sense that my finances are in order and a feeling of calm comes over me (as long as I keep within budget lol).

Pick one room and clear it. Or even one corner, like your desk. Don't you feel better? Declutter when your mind is feeling overwhelm through seeing chaos!

I HATE CHORES.
BUT SOMETIMES
YOU HAVE TO PLAY
CINDERELLA TO GET
TO THE SPARKLE.

CHAPTER SEVENTEEN

Be Budget Savvy

The next Lifestyle book will be about how to make the most of your money. In the meantime so you have more money for the things that make your heart happy, or to cut down on any debt you may be in, here's a quick round up of budgetary advice.

1. Make a spreadsheet or use a notebook to record your income and your outgoings. Keep within your means.

2. Don't borrow money unless you absolutely have to. Otherwise that £1000 for Christmas suddenly costs you a whole lot more and did your kids need 47 presents each anyway?

3. When buying large electrical items shop around for the best price on the internet. Make sure you check out reviews on the place that has the best price to make sure they are a reliable retailer. Check out

cashback sites like Quidco to see if you can purchase through them to earn cashback. I have been a member of Quidco for years and have earned over £1000 in cashback. That's right £1000. And you can convert it to Amazon vouchers at the time of writing this. How many books is that for basically buying things you intended to buy anyway.

4. Try budget brands instead of top branded items. Not every one will be a decent swap but some will and that's more savings.

5. Do you regularly have takeaway? Make your own - have a fakeaway and save money.

For every penny you save, you either become better off financially, OR you have more money for those little things like books, a new notebook, a bunch of flowers to brighten up the house, or to save for a small holiday or a family day at the beach.

DO I NEED THIS?
OR AM I TRYING
TO MEET A DESIRE
I COULD GET ANOTHER
WAY FOR LESS?

CHAPTER EIGHTEEN

FEAR
the biggest FULL STOP of your dreams

I've already told you that it stopped me from becoming self-employed for years. What is FEAR stopping you from doing?

Last month I visited the hospital to have my bloods taken and the nurse asked me what I did for a living. I told her I used to work at the exact same hospital until I almost lost my job and went self employed. She told me how much she'd like to work for herself and then she told me that she drew. Did I think people might want her illustrations for book covers?

I told her I would imagine there was a great market out there via social media for an illustrator. I told her how I edited for free at first. I advised her to do some research into it. She then told me she made dog clothes and so I told her about Etsy, and I said I bought dog coats myself from Etsy. Just try I told her, what do you have to lose? You might get that self-employment after all.

I won't ever know whether she did pursue any of this or whether FEAR held her back. Fear that her work wouldn't be good enough, that she'd get no customers. Mental obstacles stopping her from reaching for her dreams that actually don't exist.

Say she puts up an illustration and no one is interested.

Say she advertises a dog coat and nobody cares.

She tried.

Now she should look into whether she advertised in the right places, whether her prices were too high.

But maybe she wouldn't because of FEAR.

It's still happening to me now as I write this book.

What if everybody laughs and says Oh my God, did you read that pile of shit Andie wrote.

Guess what? I'm still publishing it.

Because for every Oh my God, there could be another person who says Bloody hell, Andie, did your book come at the right time for me. I felt like crawling under the duvet and never coming out until I read that. Now I'm all fired up and ready to challenge myself.

Forget other people. Forget what could go wrong. Focus on how fantastic it would be if it was successful. Go back to visualisation techniques.

ACTION

Imagine it right now. Whatever it is you want. Imagine you are successful in it right now. How does it feel? What do you need to do to make this a reality? Make a move towards that reality. Push through the FEAR. Recognise it and tell it today it's losing. YOU: 1, FEAR: 0.

(F)ACE
(E)VERYTHING
(A)ND
(R)ULE THE WORLD

CHAPTER NINETEEN

Restful moments

At times of overwhelm my mind can be bursting with what I need to do, my eyes heavy because I've stared at the computer working for far too long. Work completed, my mind and eyes exhausted, I'm like. Now what do I do?

I don't want to read because my eyes don't want more words.

When you need a break **DO** one of the following:

Listen to an audiobook.
Do some colouring (yes you can use an adult colouring book this time).
Listen to a CD.
Have a bath.
Go for a walk.
Lie back on your sofa or bed with your eyes closed (if

you fall asleep so what? If you need to go somewhere set the alarm before you close your eyes).

Do NOT go on social media. This is about having a REST. You can bet your life if you do there'll be a message from someone that needs your immediate attention and you get no rest at all.

Do NOT feel guilty about having a rest.

YEAH YOU'RE IMPORTANT
AND YOU'LL HAVE MY UNDIVIDED
ATTENTION IN THIRTY
MINUTES BECAUSE
I'M IMPORTANT TOO
AND I NEED A REST.

CHAPTER TWENTY

*It's all within you.
Go get it!*

I hope you've enjoyed my first Lifestyle book. I'd like to think it's short, yet mighty. When deciding how to set out the book I didn't feel my readers needed pages upon pages of examples and explanations. We live in a fast-paced world, attention spans are short and I could give you the information you need to be a better version of you in short, punchy chapters. The quotes you find at the end of every chapter were made up by yours truly.

Don't forget to head to the Facebook group for daily motivation. Threads will appear there where you can post your progress and success.

Find it Here

I hope to see you there. If you're not on Facebook

sign up to my newsletter which encompasses both lifestyle and my fiction. Sign up Here

All best wishes for your future happiness.

Love, Andie xoxo

YOUR DREAMS ARE
NOTHING WITHOUT
ACTION.
SHIFT YOUR ASS.

THE CALENDAR GAME

MEET THE FICTIONAL RONNIE HUNTINGTON-JONES AS
SHE MAKES OVER HER LIFE ONE HILARIOUS MONTH AT
A TIME

Ronnie Huntington-Jones is expecting a proposal
from boyfriend Col. Instead she receives a huge
shock. With best friend Stella now in New York,
Ronnie feels she needs some time for reflection and
sets herself The Calendar Game; a different project
each month to re-evaluate her life.

Finding herself with celebrity status after a
memorable Morning TV interview; Ronnie's path
crosses again with that of Harry Taylor, ex-footballer
and potentially the person who tried to kill her
in rehab.

With backstabbing, sex, lies and ladygardens, it's going to be quite a year for Ronnie. But at the end of it, will she still have love?

Buy/borrow here: The Calendar Game

ANDIE'S FICTION TITLES

THE ALPHA SERIES

The Alphabet Game
The Alphabet Wedding
The Calendar Game
The Baby Game

The Alpha Series Boxset

The Alphabet Game: Play It Playbook

THE BALL GAMES SERIES

Balls (Book One)
Snow Balls (Book Two)
New Balls Please (Book Three)
Balls Fore (Book Four)

The Ball Games Bundle (One to Four)

Jingle Balls (Book Five)
Curve Balls (Book Six)
My Book

SUPERNATURAL DATING AGENCY

The Vampire wants a Wife
A Devil of a Date

STANDALONE TITLES

UNDERNEATH
JOURNEY TO THE CENTRE OF MYSELF
SAVIOUR
MInE: Amazon
THE BUNK UP
(co-written with DH Sidebottom)

Receive **Quickies** ebook for FREE by signing up to
Andie's newsletter via Quickies

ABOUT ANDIE

Andie M. Long is author of *Amazon Number One Erotic Thrillers* **Saviour,** and **The Alphabet Game** amongst others.

She lives in Sheffield with her son and long suffering partner. When not being partner, mother, writer or editor she can usually be found on Facebook or walking her whippet, Bella.

Andie will be signing in Bristol, London and York in 2018 and Sheffield 2019.

FOLLOW ANDIE

Andie's Reader Hangout
(not a street team, just a place to hang and have fun)

Bookbub

Instagram

Amazon

Pinterest

Goodreads

mailto:contact@andiemlongwriter.com

Printed in Great Britain
by Amazon